RESTART
YOUR HEART

21 ENCOURAGING DEVOTIONS
SO YOU CAN
LOVE LIKE YOU'VE NEVER BEEN HURT

JENTEZEN FRANKLIN

Chosen
a division of Baker Publishing Group
Minneapolis, Minnesota

Published by Chosen Books
11400 Hampshire Avenue South
Bloomington, Minnesota 55438
www.chosenbooks.com

Chosen Books is a division of
Baker Publishing Group, Grand Rapids, Michigan

Printed in the United States of America

ISBN 978-0-8007-9949-6

Author represented by The FEDD Agency, Inc.

18 19 20 21 22 23 24   7 6 5 4 3 2 1

CONTENTS

CONTENTS

INTRODUCTION

THE POWER OF EXPECTATION

It's time to restart your heart. Too many of life's challenges and challenging people have filled our minds with doubt, frustration and bitterness. Check yourself by checking your self-talk. What kinds of thoughts occupy your mind these days? Are they thoughts of a hope and a future? Are they thoughts about whom you can bless and who has blessed you? Do you spend more time thinking about what you don't have than praying prayers of thanksgiving for what you do have? The conversations we have in our heads tell us a lot about the condition of our hearts. Why don't we restart those thought processes right now—today? Do you need a miracle? Do you desire a breakthrough? How about a word from God or a healing? It's time to expect great things!

Nothing can derail our pursuit of God like an offense or a hurt at the hands of another. When it comes at the hands of those we least expect to hurt us, the effects can last for years. If there is anything I have learned as a pastor, it's that time does not heal all wounds. In fact, sometimes time can be our worst enemy as that root of bitterness grows deeper, the walls go up, and the hurt turns into bitterness and isolation.

Over the next 21 days, I believe all of that can change. That *needs* to change. A restart is what is needed, and there is no time like the present to begin that process. The only requirement is expectation. Hebrews 11:6 tells us that our faith pleases God. We need to understand that if God is going to do something, He looks for people who live with great expectation. In Luke 3 we see desperate people in eager expectation of their Messiah's coming, on tiptoes in anticipation:

> Now as the people were in *expectation*, and all reasoned in their hearts about John, whether he was the Christ or not, John answered, saying to all, "I indeed baptize you with water; but One mightier than I is coming, whose sandal strap I am not worthy to loose. He will baptize you with the Holy Spirit and fire."
>
> Luke 3:15–16, emphasis added

Our God is all-powerful, yet we limit His work in our lives when we refuse to believe in His ability and His victory. We need to activate our faith and stand in tiptoe expectation, knowing He can do the impossible! Let's take a look at one man in the Bible who held great expectation.

The Lame Man at the Temple

There was a man who was lame from birth, but despite his disability, he managed to get people to carry him to the Temple to beg for money each day. His life, his livelihood and his identity revolved around his sickness. But that all changed at three o'clock one afternoon with an event that altered the trajectory of this man's life forever. The Bible tells us that Peter and John, as they were heading to the Temple, took notice of this beggar and stopped and looked intently at this spectacle of a man. The Bible says that Peter looked right at him, as did John. Then Peter said, "Look at us." So the lame man "gave them his attention, *expecting to receive something* from them" (Acts 3:4–5, emphasis added). The rest is history as that lame man was healed instantly as his feet and ankles became strong.

The man activated his faith and received his miracle right then and there because of his great expectation. What if that lame man had said to Peter and John, "I've been here every day of my life up to this point. I guess I'm just destined to be here every day from here on out." His miracle would not have taken place without his faith. He expected a gift that day—and he got a life-changing one. But, day after day, his expectation overcame his pessimism as he would awake and say, "Maybe today!"

Here's the best part of the story. He got up from that place, and, while he could have gone anywhere he wanted to go with healthy feet and ankles, he chose to go with

Peter and John to the Temple courts jumping and praising God. His heart had been restarted—and yours will be, too, as you begin to see the broken places you have learned to live with healed and made useful again.

A New Day

God has so much for you. It is no accident that you are reading these pages right now. These 21 days are a divine appointment for a surgical procedure you need. Allow the Lord to restart your heart the way He has, story after story, for readers of the companion book for this devotional, *Love Like You've Never Been Hurt* (Chosen, 2018). More than 150,000 people have read that book. Testimonies are pouring in from people who were holding on to hurt like a life preserver only to discover it was the very weight pulling them under.

Now, just like that lame beggar, it's your turn. He had his day, and his simple act of faith changed the rest of his life. It's your turn. It's your season of healing. You are one look—one touch—away from Jesus, from freedom and joy unspeakable.

You don't have to see it to believe. Start now. Praise in expectation. Sow in expectation. Pray in expectation. Expect the outpouring of the Holy Spirit in every area of your life. What area are you expecting God to break through? I want you to begin to live and speak with great expectation.

DAY 1
IT'S TIME

"This is the word of the LORD to Zerubbabel: 'Not by might nor by power, but by My Spirit,' says the LORD of hosts.

"'Who are you, O great mountain? Before Zerubbabel you shall become a plain! And he shall bring forth the capstone with shouts of "Grace, grace to it!"'"

Zechariah 4:6–7

There is a medical procedure used by heart surgeons worldwide called *cardioversion*. Cardioversion uses electricity or chemicals to activate the heart and return it to its normal rhythm. Total cardioversion involves stopping the heart and then restarting it.

An irregular heartbeat can cause great damage to internal organs, even death. Cardioversion restarts the heart, allowing it to regain its ability to do what it was designed to do, which is to supply life-giving blood to the rest of the body, in just the right measure and at the intervals required to sustain life. This amazing procedure saves thousands of lives every year.

Unforgiveness, bitterness, anger, offense, hurt and injustice can have irregular and damaging effects on our spirits. These effects disrupt our spiritual health and can harm our physical health as well. Many times, this devastation cannot be solved through usual means; the hurt is too deep. When pain is this entrenched, there is only one way back to renewed health and strength for the assignment God has for your life: You need to restart your heart.

We have to learn to love like we've never been hurt. . . . As you read these words, you may be picturing the face of the person who has caused you pain. . . . Whatever [or whoever] it is, you have loved hard and were wounded. This someone has cut off your love supply. And you are not living fully, the way God intended, because you do not know how, or if it is even possible, to love like you've never been hurt.

Love Like You've Never Been Hurt, pages 13–14

It's amazing that our minds want to dwell on the past, the film reels of our failures—those who have hurt us or rejected us, and the injustices we have experienced. I used to play those experiences over and over in my mind thinking about what I wish I had said, the things I wish I had done differently and the injustice of it all. We do this, partly, because we can't make sense of it, and our computer-like minds look for logical conclusions. But because we can't reason our way to the justice we long for, the offenses are never resolved.

And that is just where the problem lies in these endless imaginations: We try to reason through the pain, but injustice and hurt are not usually based in truth or logic or any kind of reasoning.

The Point of Attack

In my thirty-plus years of experience in ministry I have learned a profound set of truths.

1. When a problem makes no sense on a physical level, then there is something spiritual going on.

    As you spend hour after hour racking your brain for answers or trying to reason things through with someone, even with God, you find you are stuck in an endless loop that leads you back to the beginning. That's not your fault. It doesn't mean something is wrong with you. It means that you aren't dealing with reasonable people. It means that the hurt you suffered is not something you deserved, and there is no human logic that will help you rationalize it. It means that the rejection you suffered was not because of anything you did, but because some selfish soul chose to delete you from his or her life. You will never make sense of this in your mind because it is only spiritually discerned.

Let go. Shift your focus. Forgive and move on. Leave that person to the Lord to deal with, and trust that God has you, will always have you, and that His justice is on His timetable and not yours.

2. Spiritual issues will not be solved by normal means (logic, reason, justice) and must be dealt with on a spiritual level.

When pain or hurt cannot be solved through physical means, step back and take action in the spiritual realm. Pray. Forgive. Love and bless anyway. Allow the Lord to give you a greater obsession. Trust with extraordinary faith for your extraordinary situation.

This one is hard to grasp because, being human, we always want someone to blame. We want to put a face on our hurt so we can know where to direct our anger. But the fact is that our struggle is *not* against flesh and blood. "For we do not wrestle against flesh and blood, but against principalities, against powers, against the rulers of the darkness of this age, against spiritual hosts of wickedness in the heavenly places" (Ephesians 6:12). Only prayer and faith will help you with these kinds of offenses and hurts.

3. No amount of thought or planning or worry will solve a spiritual issue or a spiritual attack.

We replay the bad memories again and again. We talk about them repeatedly to anyone who will listen. We think of ways we can exact revenge. We poke and prod at our gaping wounds. In the process, we become bitter. Hardened. And, often, we withhold our love from those who need it most.

Love Like You've Never Been Hurt, page 15

Restart Your Heart

You can spend your life looking back, and many do, or you can trust God with that face you see and trust God with that injustice you have suffered, knowing that your God is not blind. *You can't fix this.* But God can fix *you*. God can create a new heart in you . . . His heart in you. And He will give you His eyes to see what He sees, His ears to hear what He hears and His heart to feel what He feels. His ways are higher, as are His thoughts, but He will give you His thoughts and His ways if you will ask for them. **13**

But before He can give you His thoughts and His ways, you have to be willing to let go of the hurt, the offense, the injustice. Let those things fall to the ground. Empty hands are required in order to receive the new thing. The old and the new cannot coexist in the same hands.

This is a lot to take in on Day 1, but if you will give yourself as an offering before God during these 21 days, He will do a work in you. You will finish as a changed person with a heart that has experienced a restart.

> [God] wants to give us a new beginning. A new story. A fresh start. He wants to heal what has been broken. He wants to reconcile what has been torn apart. . . .
>
> It is never wrong to love. It is never out of order to love. You do not compromise when you love. You never lower your standards when you love.
>
> *Love Like You've Never Been Hurt*, pages 15–16

Prayer

Lord Jesus, as I embark on this 21-day journey, help me to take every step, not with fear, but with great expectation for all You are about to do. Speak, Lord. Heal, Lord. And teach me Your timeless truths.

THE HARDEST WORDS EVER SAID

And when they had come to the place called Calvary, there they crucified Him, and the criminals, one on the right hand and the other on the left. Then Jesus said, "Father, forgive them, for they do not know what they do."

Luke 23:33–34, emphasis added

I have often wondered how Jesus was able to remain forgiving and compassionate to the very end, especially when you consider the lies, betrayal, injustice, false accusation and sheer hatred directed toward Him. I believe that the hardest words ever said by a human might possibly be these words that Jesus said just before He died on that cross: *"Forgive them, Father. They know not what they do."* But that's what love, in its purest form, does. Love is a powerful force.

Allow me to add some perspective. What if you were on that cross, and the betrayers and the accusers were children you love—either your own or other children you love and care for? Wouldn't it still be your greatest desire to see them someday forgiven and reconciled with their heavenly Father? Could you really wish to see them judged and condemned to hell? I think that must be what God saw when He looked out on all those who yelled, "Crucify Him! Crucify Him!" I don't think He saw evil. I think He saw His children—His own flesh and blood—confused, manipulated, irrational and misguided, victims of legalism run amuck.

This begs a few questions. When you hear words like *betrayal*, *false accusation*, *injustice* or *offense*, what face or faces immediately come to mind? I would venture that at least one face appears. And here is the challenge: As God looks at the names and faces in your mind, what do you think He sees? Of course, He's not blind; He saw what they did to you. But what do you think God sees? What do you think He wants *you* to see?

I have discovered that trouble is one of God's great servants because it reminds us how we need Him continually. God is not put off by your struggles. He stands ready to help you, to comfort you and to heal you. When you have reached the end of you, God is always there. He is on the mountaintop, and He is in the valley. When you are ready to throw up your hands, throw them up to Him.

God is the creator of new things. It's time to let Him give you a new beginning . . . a restart. It's time to stop limping and allow God to bind up your bruises and heal your wounds: "Moreover the light of the moon will be as the light of the sun, and the light of the sun will be sevenfold, as the light of seven days, *in the day that the LORD binds up the bruise of His people and heals the stroke of their wound*" (Isaiah 30:26, emphasis added).

Answer these simple questions and make a few decisions right where you are:

Do you want to be right or reconciled?

Do you want to be hurt or healed?

Do you want to keep being the victim or start becoming whole?

There is only one path to forgiveness. You must love like you have never been hurt. You have to be willing to say the hardest words ever said:

"Father, forgive them. They know not what they do."   **17**

"Father, forgive him. He knew not what he did."

"Father, forgive her. She simply does not understand the hurt she has caused."

"Father, forgive him. He could not possibly know the pain he caused."

"Father, forgive them. They can't possibly comprehend the pain they have caused . . . and yet, I ask You to forgive them and heal the hurt that is in me."

My guess is that there was one sentence above that resonated. Take a moment and find your sentence and think about it. Then pray on it a moment. Ask God to give you the strength and His Fatherly perspective to see that person or persons in a way you have not thought of. Ask the Lord to begin a work of forgiveness in you. More than likely this won't all be solved right now, but I challenge you to give God permission to begin a healing work in you. Ask Him to begin the work of renewing your mind for the hurt you are holding on to, and for the person who caused the pain.

The Holy Spirit will never go where He is not invited. Perhaps your greatest next step down the pathway to forgiving like you've never been hurt is in the act of giving God permission to do a new work in you.

Allow me to pray this prayer over you as you read it.

Prayer

Lord Jesus, how hard those words must have been for You to say: "Forgive them, Father, for they know not what they do." Help me to say those words in every situation, offering up those who have hurt me or someone I love. Teach me Your perspective, Lord. Help me see what You see so I can do what You want me to do. Thank You for forgiving me.

LOVE MATTERS

Though I speak with the tongues of men and of angels, but have not love, I have become sounding brass or a clanging cymbal. And though I have the gift of prophecy, and understand all mysteries and all knowledge, and though I have all faith, so that I could remove mountains, but have not love, I am nothing. And though I bestow all my goods to feed the poor, and though I give my body to be burned, but have not love, it profits me nothing.

Love suffers long and is kind; love does not envy; love does not parade itself, is not puffed up; does not behave rudely, does not seek its own, is not provoked, thinks no evil; does not rejoice in iniquity, but rejoices in the truth; bears all things, believes all things, hopes all things, endures all things.

Love never fails.

1 Corinthians 13:1–8, emphasis added

My frustration mounted, but my heart broke. Arguments like this one had taken place many times, it seemed, not just with this daughter, but with others as well.

During that particular episode, we were smack in the middle of a family crisis. Each day brought another fight. Some clashes were more disruptive than others. Some aroused deep sadness. Others harsh words.

Love Like You've Never Been Hurt, page 20

Every family has been there. Maybe you are there right now. Family conflict is the worst, especially if you are the parent. You just want peace and harmony with the people you care more about than anyone in the world. You want your home to be a place filled with laughter and amazing memories, but no family is perfect and no home is immune to conflict. We have conflict because we are imperfect people trying to coexist with other imperfect people.

It has been said that family provides us with life's greatest joys and deepest sorrows. Conflict, when it goes unresolved, hardens the heart over time and builds walls where there were once bridges. Add a marriage to the mix, two imperfect people who many times look at the same situation differently, and you have the makings of a perfect storm. The friction that can occur in any discussion about what to do can sometimes add even more conflict and division. Satan's strategy has never changed: divide and conquer. A house divided cannot stand.

Meanwhile, life and the world we live in don't shut down and wait for our lives to get back to normal. In fact, if your situation is the way mine was, while the walls are caving in at home you may be enjoying great success in your professional life. When we were going through our toughest times, our ministry was exploding and expanding at a record pace. But it can be very difficult to put on the professional face and paint on a smile when the things that matter most are falling apart. Try standing in front of thousands of people and delivering a word from God when there is hell at home. It's at times like these that you feel the weakest and most vulnerable. But I have a few things to share that will encourage you.

In This Season

Here are five encouraging lessons for seasons of conflict.

First, I have discovered an astonishing truth: God is attracted to weakness. When we are empty vessels, He longs to fill us with His grace, love and goodness. This is good news. An empty vessel is what God desires so He can fill you with what you will need for the season you are in. In times when there is great stress or conflict you need extra doses of grace, love and goodness. You *have* faith for this.

Second, I have great news: It's a season . . . not a sentence. This too shall pass, and when the storm has passed, only the harshest of words spoken will be remembered. So when you are in the heat of the moment, it is critical that you guard your tongue: "Death and life are in the power of the tongue" (Proverbs 18:21).

Today, several years after our toughest seasons, all of our children love and follow Jesus, and our relationships are strong. The memories are still as vivid as ever, but they no longer have any power over our lives. Now they serve as lessons and roadmaps for others who are in the thick of their storms.

Third, the pain you feel is the pain you can heal. As a pastor I never worry so much about the people who are feeling the pain of their situation, because where there is pain, there is attention, and the more specific the source of the pain, the easier it is to focus your attention and your prayers. It's the people who have grown so spiritually dull that they cannot even feel the pain they are causing that I worry about. Ask God to reveal, specifically, where the source of the pain is. All remedies begin and end at the root. Find the root and you solve the crisis.

Fourth, never underestimate the power of being in God's house. Even when you don't want to go . . . go. Even if you have kids who don't want to go . . . go. Even if it seems that the Word of God isn't getting in and penetrating their hearts—or yours—it is. God's Word *never* returns void (see Isaiah 55:11).

Besides the Word of God, there are also the people of God—relationships that develop when people are together week after week over an extended period of time. And you never know when there will be that breakthrough moment.

These moments eventually happened for my children, and it was largely because the people of God loved on them, prayed for them, mentored them and spoke life into them. If you are going through a storm in your home, stay in God's house.

Lastly, and most important of all, never forget, *love matters*. It really does. "And above all things have fervent love for one another, for 'love will cover a multitude of sins'" (1 Peter 4:8).

A New Language

Love *does* cover a multitude of sins and speaks a language all its own. In everything we went through as a family and in every stressful conflict, down deep, my kids knew we loved them. They knew that even though there were disagreements, deep disagreements, everything we did or said came from a place of love.

Love prays without ceasing. Love fasts. Love lays our children in the hands of the Lord daily. Love stays the course in the things that matter most, no matter the conflict it causes. Love stays in God's house, love stays on its knees, and love never lets go. Love believes the best, and love has faith for the promises in God's Word in spite of the current circumstances. Love matters. Always has. Always will.

Life is an adventure in forgiveness. It's all about releasing the past and reaching for the future. And I know of only one way to do this: Love like you have never been hurt.

Prayer

Lord Jesus, teach me to love as You love with unconditional love. And thank You for loving me. Help me to be more loving, not just to those who love me back, but to everyone You bring across my path. Thank You, Lord, for Your everlasting love.

LOVE NEVER FAILS

Yet in all these things we are more than conquerors through Him who loved us. For I am persuaded that neither death nor life, nor angels nor principalities nor powers, nor things present nor things to come, nor height nor depth, nor any other created thing, shall be able to separate us from the love of God which is in Christ Jesus our Lord.

Romans 8:37–39

We just do not know how to love—all the time. Oh, we can love when we agree with one another. . . . We can love when we share the same lifestyle. We can even love strangers or those who don't know us well. But it sure is harder to love those who are closest to us. Why? Because they can hurt us the most.

Love Like You've Never Been Hurt, page 29

Love wins! Love wins all the time. Love never fails. I think that we forget too easily that the love we have for others is of a different kind. When you surrendered your life to Christ, the Holy Spirit set up residence inside you, and from that moment on you were given a new DNA, a new heart and access to a new kind of love. "Or do you not know that your body is the temple of the Holy Spirit who is in you, whom you have from God, and you are not your own? For you were bought at a price; therefore glorify God in your body and in your spirit, which are God's" (1 Corinthians 6:19–20).

When we make Jesus the center of our lives, we become part of a bloodline that sees hurt and offense differently because we see others differently. We love with a different kind of love. So when offense and setbacks come, if we look closely and ask God for His eyes, we see each situation differently from the way the world sees it, and the work of forgiveness can plant a seed and begin to take root.

The flesh will cry out for justice, but the spirit will trust that God sees, God hears, and God will make it work for good and His glory in the end. But I'm the first to admit that this kind of love is not easy, and rarely my first instinct. My first impulse is to strike back and go on the offensive. But that is just what I said it was—my first impulse. I have learned over the years that I cannot let my first impulse be my first response. I have learned that in those moments when my blood is boiling or the cut is the deepest, I must do what David learned to do . . . step back, take a deep breath and inquire of the Lord (see 1 Samuel 30:8).

Focus Is Everything

I can tell you with great confidence that in every situation of great offense or personal attack that, however I chose to respond, God was always waiting in that place where my eyes lifted off my circumstances and turned to look to Him. Every time my focus shifted, He was there, and He will do the same for you. His love never fails. I am always amazed at how near He is. And His solution is always the same . . . love.

Love is a weapon that can shatter division and rebuild what is broken. These are hard choices to make, especially in the heat of the battle or the attack, but if you will make these choices you will make room for God to do in the supernatural what you could never do in the natural.

Maybe you know well the sting of hatred or resentment. Maybe a close friend abandoned you because he or she was jealous. Instead of encouraging you, believing in you, this person cut you off. I want to remind you that when Joseph's world turned upside down, when all hope seemed dried up, he held on.

Love Like You've Never Been Hurt, page 32

Perhaps the greatest revelation you can receive on the topic of offense and forgiveness is this: In every situation, and no matter how helpless you feel, you always have a choice of how to respond. Unforgiveness is like drinking poison and expecting it to affect the person you refuse to forgive. The only person it hurts is you. *Choose love over hurt.*

Forgiveness may not come immediately; in fact, that is rarely the case. But love *can* come immediately because it's a choice, and a choice no one can take from you. Better yet, it's the best choice; it's the choice God desires and rewards. That's a powerful promise! Choose to love others—always.

Press On

This next point is critical to the call and purpose God has for your life: No matter the offense or hurt, choose to keep pressing forward. So many times these situations can be paralyzing. Sometimes in my family, our greatest and most hurtful conflicts would happen just moments before I had to go to the church to preach before thousands of people. Those conversations with God on the way to the church would talk me out of quitting right then and there or from turning that car around and going back home.

Pressing forward was a choice, but it was a choice birthed in obedience to God's voice in those difficult seasons. Never forget that there is an enemy who comes to kill and destroy—and his tactic is always deception, because he is a liar. He will whisper defeat and indignation and condemnation with one purpose in mind: to get you to turn away from God and His purposes and His call on your life. Satan wants to kill your dream and cancel your assignment. Don't give in.

When you're going through hell, don't stop there. Keep moving forward.

Choose to keep driving toward the goal the Lord has set before you. Rebuke those voices of defeat and condemnation in Jesus' name and fix your gaze fully forward. Keep moving. Don't give in and don't stand still in those moments. The devil knows if he can cease your forward momentum there is a chance you will turn and go back.

When the trials and conflicts of this life come, there will almost always be a face and a name associated with the attack. Don't give in to your first impulse. Step back and inquire of the Lord. Love *always* wins. Choose to love others—always. Keep pressing forward, even when you feel weak. It is a great spiritual truth that when we are at our weakest He is strong on our behalf.

And never forget that your circumstances are never intimidating to your God. Draw near to the God who is always so much nearer than you might have imagined. God wants to heal you and defend you and even avenge you if you will simply draw near. Do that now.

Prayer

Lord God, thank You for Your unfailing love. Thank You that even when I fall down or fail, You don't withhold Your love for me. Teach me to love like that, Lord. Help me not to place restrictions on my love and to love even those who have hurt me. Thank You for Your patience and Your careful, guiding hand in my life, Lord.

PUSHING PAST THE QUITTING POINTS

"'Fear not, for I am with you; be not dismayed, for I am your God. I will strengthen you, yes, I will help you, I will uphold you with My righteous right hand.' . . .

"You shall seek them and not find them—those who contended with you. Those who war against you shall be as nothing, as a nonexistent thing."

Isaiah 41:10, 12

I'm not saying it's going to be easy. It's a process, sometimes a long one. As Christians, we want the instantaneous. We are a microwave generation that craves solutions to problems in thirty seconds flat. News flash: While God certainly does perform instantaneous deliverance, that is the exception, not the norm.

So pray and keep praying. Believe and keep believing. Forgive and keep forgiving. . . . Get wisdom from godly counsel. Do what it takes to heal the wound.

Love Like You've Never Been Hurt, pages 37–38

In short: Don't give up. Don't give in. Your family, your purpose, your calling—all are worth fighting for. You have to learn that your weapons are not physical, but they are mighty, and they will see you through those times when you want to give up or give in. There were so many times when we were dealing with our kids in the teenage years that it would have been so easy just to step aside and let them go make their messes. But that was not the role God gave me as their earthly father. The easiest way is seldom the wisest way. There are times you have to stand your ground when everything in you is ready to give in.

When bad times become unbearable, step back and let the Lord fight for you. Every day, life happens! You've been there. I've been there. Everyone has experienced some level of frustration and pain amid the daily throngs of life. No one is immune to the realities of life. That begs the question, "What do you do when Bad Times turn into

Unbearable Times?" The answer to that question eludes far too many of us, even in the Christian world. Why? Because we have all made the naïve and foolish statement, "Can things get any worse?"

If you have ever uttered such a sentiment, you are in good company. The children of Israel made the same declaration. Moses and Aaron had asked the power hungry Pharaoh to let God's people leave for a few days of worship out in the desert. Sounds like a reasonable request. But the outcome produced more hurt and difficulty for the children of God than they had ever known.

> The same day Pharaoh commanded the taskmasters of the people and their officers, saying, "You shall no longer give the people straw to make brick as before. Let them go and gather straw for themselves. And you shall lay on them the quota of bricks which they made before. You shall not reduce it. For they are idle; therefore they cry out, saying, 'Let us go and sacrifice to our God.' Let more work be laid on the men, that they may labor in it, and let them not regard false words."
>
> Exodus 5:6–9

In an instant, an already bad situation now became unbearable! Ever had a day like that? A month like that? A year like that? Do you have an overloaded life demanding more from you? Do you have relationships that continue to make withdrawals without deposits? Do you find yourself in the depths of your soul asking God how you can keep your head above water?

Drowning lives get God's attention, and drowning people give more attention to God.

I am sure you can identify with the Hebrew people in this timeless story. Bad yesterday! Today unbearable! But what happens next is usually life changing. "Then the Lord said to Moses, 'Now you shall see what I will do to Pharaoh. For with a strong hand he will let them go, and with a strong hand he will drive them out of his land'" (Exodus 6:1).

When we become desperate, we cry out in desperation, which is an entirely different kind of prayer. Desperate cries for help create divine deliverance and will push you through those quitting places. God heard the cries of His people and moved on their behalf. He will do this in your circumstances as well. The next time you find yourself in a desperate and unbearable situation, consider the following:

Relax: "Return to your rest, O my soul, for the Lord has dealt bountifully with you" (Psalm 116:7).

Cast: "Therefore humble yourselves under the mighty hand of God, that He may exalt you in due time, casting all your care upon Him, for He cares for you" (1 Peter 5:6–7).

Rest: "My soul, wait silently for God alone, for my expectation is from Him" (Psalm 62:5). "The fear of the LORD leads to life; then one rests content, untouched by trouble" (Proverbs 19:23 NIV).

Those three words, *relax*, *cast* and *rest*, describe productive actions you can take when life goes sideways. *Relax*—God is working things out for your good in spite of what you see happening around you. *Cast*—Like casting a fishing line far from the bank, God wants you to cast your troubles far from the bank of your soul. *Rest*—Contented resting, untouched by trouble, is available for you in the midst of the unbearable times.

Today set aside time to consider the challenging decisions or circumstances you are facing. Grab a piece of paper and write them down. Place them in order of weight or heaviness on your heart. Try to limit the number to the top three. One by one, spend time in prayer asking God to help you to *relax in Him, cast off the concern and rest over the outcome*. He's a *big* God, and He can provide *big* comfort, hope and ultimately peace in the middle of the storm. When bad becomes unbearable, God will always be there, waiting for your eyes to lift off your circumstances and rest in His unfailing gaze.

Never give up. Never give in. Push past those quitting points. It is always darkest before the dawn. Joy comes in the morning!

Prayer

Dear Lord, You know where I am weak and where I lack the resolve I need for every situation. Be near me, Lord, I pray, especially on those days when I feel as if I cannot go on. Help me push past the quitting points in my life. Make them markers that remind me of those days when You helped me overcome.

IT IS NEVER WRONG TO LOVE

"But if you love those who love you, what credit is that to you? For even sinners love those who love them. And if you do good to those who do good to you, what credit is that to you? For even sinners do the same. And if you lend to those from whom you hope to receive back, what credit is that to you? For even sinners lend to sinners to receive as much back. But love your enemies, do good, and lend, hoping for nothing in return; and your reward will be great, and you will be sons of the Most High. For He is kind to the unthankful and evil. Therefore be merciful, just as your Father also is merciful."

Luke 6:32–36

If those we love are doing something that is wrong, often our judgment kicks into overdrive. Disapproval quickly trumps love. We refuse to have anything to do with those people. We announce to them and to the world that the relationship is over. And we do this in the name of faith, thumping our Bibles with self-righteous intolerance. . . . We could have all the spiritual gifts in the world, but without love, they would be meaningless.

Love Like You've Never Been Hurt, page 46

I want to be clear. Loving unconditionally does not mean lowering your standards. We all face the struggle between not wanting to condone someone's behavior but yet loving that person through it. In *Love Like You've Never Been Hurt*, I talk about my friend Mac when his son told him that he was gay. What do you do in that situation? What do you do if it's not somebody else's relative . . . it's your own flesh and blood. The answer is simple and it is constant: You love. It is *never* wrong to love another.

Love Anyway

Loving unconditionally doesn't mean lowering your standards, but it also doesn't mean you are judge and jury. Only God is the ultimate authority when it comes to sin and judgment. True love acknowledges that there is a sin problem, but it also says that your love is not subject to the approval of someone's behavior or decisions or lifestyle. **39**

I have often thought to myself how hard it must be for God, the ultimate Father, to create a human being—someone He loves with a love like no other—and then to watch as, bit by bit, He sees His child turn a silent back toward Him, choose not to acknowledge Him or, worse yet, decide to reject Him. But the father in me understands what it means to say that there isn't anything that could ever cause me to stop loving my children. Nothing. And so it is with God.

All that to say that every human being ever created was God's idea and His creation. So don't be surprised if He doesn't see that person who hurt you quite the same as you do. Parents can care about other people's children, but their love for someone else's kids will never be the same as the love they have for their own. Each person you encounter in conflict or disappointment is a person that the heavenly Father desperately wants you to reconcile with. And reconciliation, according to 2 Corinthians, is our primary calling.

> For the love of Christ compels us, because we judge thus: that if One died for all, then all died; and He died for all, that those who live should live no longer for themselves, but for Him who died for them and rose again. Therefore, from now on, we regard no one according to the flesh. Even though we have known Christ according to the flesh, yet now we know Him thus no longer. Therefore, if anyone is in Christ, he is a new creation; old things have passed away; behold, all things have become new. Now all things are of God, who has reconciled us to Himself through Jesus Christ, and has given us the ministry of reconciliation, that

is, that God was in Christ reconciling the world to Himself, not imputing their trespasses to them, and has committed to us the word of reconciliation. Now then, we are ambassadors for Christ, as though God were pleading through us: we implore you on Christ's behalf, be reconciled to God.

2 Corinthians 5:14–20

Allow me to take a different tack. What would your life look like if God did not respond to your weaknesses, your sins, your addictions or your failures with grace and love? In fact, His Word says it even stronger than that: "If you forgive men their trespasses, your heavenly Father will also forgive you. But if you do not forgive men their trespasses, neither will your Father forgive your trespasses" (Matthew 6:14–15). It is truly a game changer when I realize that forgiveness for my sins requires that I forgive others their sins, even when those sins bring harm to me or mine.

Sometimes You Love from a Distance

The last topic I would like for you to consider before you begin your prayer time has to do with situations where loving must be done in safety. You can love in your heart, willing and praying for the good of others—from a distance.

Being a Christian does not mean you have to be a punching bag for God, a doormat or a crash test dummy.

This does not mean that they have drifted beyond the reach of God. It just means that there are some gaps that only God can narrow, and, in those cases, those people need to go through God before they can be with you.

Be kind but firm in creating that space, and think of ways to connect without being together physically. Use wisdom, especially if children are involved. You can make room in your heart while also maintaining healthy physical boundaries. Love, love, love always, but be wise when it comes to the personal safety of you or any children who might be affected.

Loving others, even when you are hurt, is a decision, and it is always the right decision. When hurt comes in the form of someone close to you choosing the path of sin, it can be incredibly painful. Remember to leave the judging to God, but love unconditionally. It is *never* wrong to love and extend love. And never forget: That person who has created the offense or the distance or the pain is a person your Savior loves intensely and died for. Sometimes perspective is everything. See others through the eyes of their Creator, and allow God to show you what He sees.

Prayer

Lord Jesus, thank You for reminding me that it is never wrong to love. Make me more loving, Lord. I open my mind and my heart to Your perfect will. Show me the faces, Lord, the faces of those that I am not being loving toward. Teach me and show me and help me, Lord, I pray.

DON'T SETTLE; KEEP CLIMBING

Therefore we also, since we are surrounded by so great a cloud of witnesses, let us lay aside every weight, and the sin which so easily ensnares us, and let us run with endurance the race that is set before us, looking unto Jesus, the author and finisher of our faith, who for the joy that was set before Him endured the cross, despising the shame, and has sat down at the right hand of the throne of God.

For consider Him who endured such hostility from sinners against Himself, lest you become weary and discouraged in your souls.

Hebrews 12:1–3

Don't speak to the fool in others; speak to the king in them. . . . I believe inside every one of us is a king. I liken this to our potential to be the people God created us to be through Christ Jesus. We may struggle. But there is a king within us. We may fail. But there is a king within us. We may not be who we can be. But there is a king within us. Often, it is not easy to see the king or the queen in our home.

Love Like You've Never Been Hurt, pages 56–57

If we really understood who we are and what Jesus thinks about us, it would change everything. We too often blend in with the world rather than acknowledge that we are children of the King, joint heirs and a royal priesthood. We have a hard time getting our minds around just how much we are loved by our heavenly Father. If we struggle with this true identity, we will struggle when conflict comes. Anxiety replaces faith, and worry displaces the confidence a child of the King should have.

But I praise God for His patience, grace and mercy. Even when I shrink in the face of adversity and allow my mind to imagine the worst, here comes Jesus, reaching out His hand and rescuing me from the demise I have envisioned.

Isn't it amazing that God can move on our behalf and, in a moment of crisis, come through with just the right answer or provision for that hour? And then, isn't it even more amazing when He does it again . . . and again . . .

and again?

But as amazing as this is, I find it even more astonishing that when we go through the *next* major crisis, we suffer from amnesia and forget all the times He has come through for us in the past. Rather than remember God's legacy of faithfulness, we ponder our physical limitations and surface circumstances. We choose human logic over divine prayer and turn back in discouragement because we know we just settled for less than God's best.

Satan is the great deceiver. If he can create just enough doubt, then he can set up a stronghold that keeps us from the high place that God has called us to. Then there we are, paralyzed with fear of the unknown, and all progress stops.

What's Next?

How easy it is to settle right where we are, in the land of the "familiar" rather than take the risk of climbing higher! We can know that we know that God is calling us to that next place . . . that next step in the journey. We can trust Him to lead us where we have never gone. We can believe that God has a plan in every stormy situation and false accusation. And we can embrace that plan to make us stronger for everything He is about to do.

It takes courage to love those who hurt or offend us. Climbing higher is not a simple task, especially when it would be so easy just to take the normal way out and isolate and avoid. Don't settle for going only halfway up the mountain. Keep climbing. Keep forgiving. Keep loving. You have to realize that many times your next step or next assignment is linked directly to your response to the last hurt or offense.

You Have a Legacy

The DNA of tried and tested faith is your legacy. God is calling you to do even greater things than you did before, maybe in a different field, in a different way or a different place—but you're going higher not lower. You need to believe that as you go up, the strongholds are coming down in Jesus' name. Never trust the flesh in matters of faith. Rather than count the cost, remember who you are: a child of the King, and He is calling you upward.

Maybe you are going through something that seems *impossible*. But hasn't God come through in your life time and time again? Take inventory. Remember God's legacy. He will not let you down. Take that next step of faith. Take that risk. Make that phone call. Plan on that mountain to be moved . . . *soon*!

Forgiveness is tough. There is going to be conflict because we see things from different perspectives. But we do not have to go through the challenges of life with fear or anxiety. "Trust in the LORD with all your heart, and lean not on your own understanding; in all your ways acknowledge Him, and He *shall* direct your paths" (Proverbs 3:5–6, emphasis added).

It's a promise. Fear not. Steady on. And watch the Lord come through just as He has again and again. Choose to love. Choose to forgive. Don't stop climbing.

Prayer

Lord Jesus, forgive me for the urge to settle and not reach for Your best. Help me keep climbing, no matter how steep the mountain or how slow the progress. Teach me to draw my strength from You, Lord, and make me stronger for the journey.

STOP KEEPING SCORE AND START LOSING COUNT

Then Peter came to Him and said, "Lord, how often shall my brother sin against me, and I forgive him? Up to seven times?"

Jesus said to him, "I do not say to you, up to seven times, but up to seventy times seven."

Matthew 18:21–22

Maybe you feel my pain. I do not know your skill set, but I do know that, no matter how bad we are at math, most of us are good at keeping score when it comes to people who have caused us harm.

Some of us even have photographic memories when it comes to holding a grudge. We know exactly the year, the month and the precise time of day of every single offense that has come our way. We create mental spreadsheets for each person who has hurt us and start tallying up marks for every offense. . . .

No matter how many times we have been hurt, the Bible is clear on one thing: We must forgive.

Love Like You've Never Been Hurt, page 63

We have talked about love, the need to forgive and about pressing on in the face of adversity, but there is another test we are called to take, and it's a math test. I know that with just about every new offense, there is a familiar face. Sometimes I work through an offense and think I really have forgiven the person who hurt me. I'm even as pleasant as possible if we happen to meet in a social or work situation. But as soon as there is a new offense from that person, it's not just a new offense; it's the fifth time, by golly! And I pull up that lengthy record of wrongs and throw the entire book at the one who hurt me. It's human nature.

The problem is that we are not called to live according to human nature. We have a higher calling with a higher

49

level of math. This math starts with Peter's generous suggestion that $7 \times 1 = 0$. But Jesus took it to a whole new level and declared that $70 \times 7 = 0$ as well. And I am reminded all over again of that passage in Isaiah that really explains everything you need to know about the way the Lord thinks and acts: "'For My thoughts are not your thoughts, nor are your ways My ways,' says the LORD. 'For as the heavens are higher than the earth, so are My ways higher than your ways, and My thoughts than your thoughts'" (Isaiah 55:8–9).

The God we serve says to love our enemies and go the extra mile. He says to work as if He is our employer and as if He is watching all the time—because He is. The God we serve asks for ten percent of our income and all of our Sunday mornings. And when it comes to forgiveness, He simply asks of us the very thing we ask of Him: forgiveness. Over and over and over again.

If you want to learn to love like you have never been hurt, you must forgive.

> Forgiveness is not about keeping score. It's about losing count. We are all going to get hurt in some way. . . . While getting hurt is reality, getting and staying bitter is a reaction. We must live a lifestyle of constant forgiveness.
>
> *Love Like You've Never Been Hurt*, page 64

This is not, of course, about satisfying the requirements of a mathematical equation. We must forgive. *All* the time.

As C. S. Lewis noted so aptly, "Everyone thinks forgiveness is a lovely idea until he has something to forgive."

It's Literally Unforgiveable Not to Forgive

"If you forgive men their trespasses, your heavenly Father will also forgive you. But if you do not forgive men their trespasses, neither will your Father forgive your trespasses" (Matthew 6:14–15). I don't know about you, but this passage of Scripture hits me right between the eyes every time. And if you are anything like me, you really do try to forgive. But on dark days when everything is going wrong, it seems that those times of injustice or offense or accusation play like a broken record or a highlight reel in living color—presenting those moments over and over in your head. You are there again. You feel it all over again as if it happened yesterday.

I remember a scene in a movie one time when a man was struggling with forgiveness for something another man had done to his child—something awful. While I don't remember much about the movie, I do remember the words this man spoke as he was locked in the struggle with God between the injustice of what had happened and God's command to forgive. It took me completely by surprise when he didn't ask for the strength to forgive or for divine help to forgive. Instead of wrestling with the words of forgiveness, he said these simple but profound words: *Heal me.*

Heal Me, Lord

One of the most amazing discoveries you will ever make in the hardest situations to forgive is that you don't need a magical formula or the right words. In those moments of deepest pain, you need to ask God to heal that broken part of you. At the hands of the Great Physician true healing can begin—and it usually starts with the eyes. He begins to show you a different way to see the situation. You experience peace that only the touch of God can bring. *Heal me, Lord. Heal the parts of me that keep me from forgiving.*

I have come to learn that healing and forgiveness are one and the same when it comes to restoration and having the heart of God for that soul who has hurt me deeply.

Don't ever be afraid to be real and speak the truth about what is in you and what is missing when you talk with God. If you read the Psalms you will find that David was as real and as brutally honest as he could possibly be . . . and God loved that. It was David's deepest honesty that produced his greatest songs; his greatest tragedies that led to his greatest victories. And in the end, God said he was a man after His own heart.

I want to be that person. I want you to be that person. If there are hurts that have cut so deeply that you can't find forgiveness to give, ask instead for that first step in the process. Ask God to heal the broken places. Ask Him to heal your "forgiver." And then watch to see Him do an amazing work in your life. Forgiveness *is* possible.

Prayer

Lord Jesus, please help me change the way I see the faces of those who represent offense or hurt. Help me instead to see these as the faces of people You want me to love. Help me to see what You see. Help me to shift my focus off my past and onto the present and the future You have planned for my life. And for those closest to me, Lord, help me to stop keeping score. Help me to begin anew in each relationship.

THE BEST BROUGHT OUT BY THE WORST

Now He who searches the hearts knows what the mind of the Spirit is, because He makes intercession for the saints according to the will of God.

And we know that all things work together for good to those who love God, to those who are the called according to His purpose.

Romans 8:27–28

[Sometimes,] the best in us can only be brought out by the worst done to us. We do not like what happened to us. It hurt. It broke our hearts. But the truth is that sometimes the best in you will never be released until the worst has been done to you. And usually it will be done by people whom you have loved, trusted and helped the most. God does not intend for the painful experiences in your life to destroy you.

Love Like You've Never Been Hurt, page 67

Resistance gives us lift. It is the principle by which every airplane flies. Hurtful words, betrayal, false accusation and other difficult experiences in life can teach us or simply reveal us. If you are still embittered when you hear that person's name or cannot stop thinking about what happened, chances are you have not forgiven that person. You have more work to do.

Sometimes the contents of forgiveness take time to come together. Sometimes a little at a time is all you can do. Start there. Pray and pray some more. Ask God to heal those broken places as we discussed yesterday. Keep praying. Keep taking that high road. Keep loving, even if it's from a distance. "Ask, and it will be given to you; seek, and you will find; knock, and it will be opened to you. For everyone who asks receives, and he who seeks finds, and to him who knocks it will be opened" (Matthew 7:7–8).

God isn't out to try to confuse you or see you get beaten up. He is for you. His plans are to prosper you. He has an assignment with your name on it. He never sleeps because He never stops thinking about you. If you are struggling with forgiveness, He isn't waiting, pencil in hand, to grade you *F* and disqualify you. He is there to help you be set free from the chains of unforgiveness. Keep asking. Keep seeking. Keep knocking. Forgiveness will come if you don't give up.

> Research has consistently shown links between the mind and body. What we think about manifests physically. According to the Mayo Clinic, holding a grudge has a negative effect on the cardiovascular and nervous systems. One study has shown that people who thought about an offense regularly experienced high blood pressure, elevated heart rates and increased muscle tensions.
>
> On the contrary, here is what you get when you forgive: healthier relationships, greater spiritual and psychological well-being, less anxiety, lower blood pressure, fewer symptoms of depression, a stronger immune system and improved heart health. Seems like a pretty good deal. And a no-brainer.
>
> *Love Like You've Never Been Hurt*, page 71

A great Bible character example is Elijah the prophet. He had so many miraculous experiences that you would think his faith would be unshakable. He caused the rain to stop for three years (see 1 Kings 17:1; 18:1), had all of his physical needs supplied by God Himself (see 1 Kings

17:4), prophesied a bottomless jar of flour and oil (see 1 Kings 17:14) and beat the prophets of Baal by calling down fire from heaven (see 1 Kings 18:38).

Then just moments after leading one of the greatest defeats in the history of prophets, we find him running for his life in fear of King Ahab and his angry wife, Jezebel. She vowed that he would die that day. Elijah chose to respond to the threat rather than rely on the victory. After running as far and for as long as he could, he found himself in the hot desert, all alone and feeling abandoned by the God he served.

But even in the harsh heat and wind of the desert, even though he was a fugitive on the run, God met him there. God fed him there, gave him water and allowed him to rest. Better yet, after Elijah had rested and voiced all his complaints, he finally calmed down enough to hear God's voice. With a still, small voice the Lord spoke to the prophet that day (see 1 Kings 19:12).

Our lives are that way. If you look back you can see victories and defeats. And it is a daily struggle to train our minds to focus just as much on the wins as we do on the losses. Our minds want to walk right past twenty victories to get to that one embarrassing defeat and sit down and dwell on it. We see only the individual who has wronged us and focus on the hurt rather than any good we can find.

Focus Matters

Where we focus matters. What we focus on has a profound physical effect on our bodies. This challenges us to choose wisely the things we dwell on. I think this is why Scripture is so clear about keeping our thoughts in check.

> For the weapons of our warfare are not carnal but mighty in God for pulling down strongholds, casting down arguments and every high thing that exalts itself against the knowledge of God, *bringing every thought into captivity* to the obedience of Christ.
>
> 2 Corinthians 10:4–5, emphasis added

As you go through your day today, check yourself. Are you thinking about your amazing future? Or are you replaying disappointments and hurts and failures of the past? Sometime the person I need to forgive the most is me! I can take you to just about every major failure I have experienced. Those memories are far too easy to retrieve. But I have to take those thoughts captive, lay them at the foot of the cross and ask the Lord to fill my mind with hope for the future. And so do you.

Prayer

Father God, help me to see every trial and every challenge as a chance to grow. Help me to see Your plan in every difficult situation, knowing You are working it out for my good. Help me never to forget that You are with me always.

THE STRUGGLE IS REAL

Bearing with one another, and forgiving one another, if anyone has a complaint against another; even as Christ forgave you, so you also must do.

Colossians 3:13

I have noticed that when people struggle with unforgiveness, it shows. This is an absolute: Hold on to a grievance or hate as if your life depended on it, and I will show you emotional, spiritual and even physical decay. . . . The weight of unforgiveness will drag you down. It is too heavy a load to carry in the race you are called to run.

Love Like You've Never Been Hurt, page 71

One of the greatest examples of forgiveness under duress is Corrie ten Boom. In *Clippings from My Notebook* (Nelson, 1982), writing of World War II and the Holocaust she endured, she puts it like this:

Forgiveness holds the key to freedom, healing, and wholeness. Wherever you release forgiveness, you release the power of the Spirit of God and the power of healing. . . . Forgiveness is the key that unlocks the door of resentment and the handcuffs of hatred. It is a power that breaks the chains of bitterness and the shackles of selfishness.

The story of Corrie ten Boom and her Dutch family, told in *The Hiding Place* (Chosen, 1971), is loved all over the world. She and her family were arrested by Nazis for harboring hundreds of Jews during the Holocaust. These were words she wrote after the terrible treatment she and her sister received in the Ravensbrück concentration camp, where her sister suffered till she died. Other family members died in prison. The things man has done to man over the centuries are both alarming and profoundly sad. And yet, in the midst of Corrie's hellish experience, we see a bright and shining example of loving like you have never been hurt. The struggle is real, but so are the blessings.

What's Stopping You?

If you are still unable to forgive someone at Day 10 of this devotional, then there is a strong possibility you are either struggling with a callous heart or you or someone you love dearly was hurt deeply. Allow me to add some context for a few things that forgiveness does *not* mean.

Forgiveness Does Not Mean You Have to Forget

"Forgive and forget" is a common misconception. There are things that happen to us, good and bad, that we could not possibly forget. That is normal. God sent me to you here today to relieve you of that false expectation. He removes sin as far as the east is from the west, but forgetting is not a requirement.

Forgiveness Will Help You Remember Differently

Instead of [your bad memory] serving as a GPS coordinate for bitterness, the offense will eventually become a point of reference for how far you have come in the healing process and how much God has worked in your life to see beyond the hurt. Forgiving someone may be instantaneous, but the healing work takes time.

Love Like You've Never Been Hurt, page 75

Forgiveness Does Not Release the Offender from Consequences

When extremely hurtful things are done to us, we can feel strong resistance to forgive because we think that if we forgive, then they get away with it. Justice matters to God as much or more than it does to us. Our first instinct will be to avenge or to seek revenge. But may I tell you about a myth that many people think is in the Bible? The Bible does *not* teach an eye for an eye. In fact, it teaches the opposite.

> "You have heard that it was said, 'An eye for an eye and a tooth for a tooth.' But I tell you not to resist an evil person. But whoever slaps you on your right cheek, turn the other to him also. If anyone wants to sue you and take away your tunic, let him have your cloak also. And whoever compels you to go one mile, go with him two."
>
> Matthew 5:38–41

Forgiveness Does Not Always Mean Reconciliation

This is a big one. Do you sometimes worry that if you choose to forgive, then you are obligated to reconcile and act as if nothing ever happened? This is not the case. Never let this be your excuse for not forgiving. Just do it and trust God with what comes next. Release that person from the prison of your making. Remember that to forgive or not to forgive is, and has always been, a decision. Choose to forgive.

Forgiveness Defined

The word *forgive* in Greek is *aphiemi*, which means literally "to send away." Forgiveness, then, is the refusal to continue carrying an offense and deciding instead to send it away. It has been said that, "Forgiveness is setting someone free and discovering that it is you who was captive." Withholding forgiveness is one of the largest obstacles we can put in between ourselves and the fullness of joy. Send it away.

In my life when I am struggling to forgive, it affects everything. I'm not present in the moment because my mind keeps returning to the time when I was hurt. I'm not as kind because I feel weighed down by the burden I carry. I'm not as thoughtful because I'm obsessed with how I have been wronged and my thirst for justice. And I don't want the best for others because I believe I am "owed" something.

But when I forgive and send it away . . . I am free.

Send it away right now. Choose to release and forgive and loosen the grip that unforgiveness has on you. Right now.

Prayer

Lord Jesus, be ever near me on those days when I am struggling to forgive. Help me control my tongue when everything in me wants to lash out and hurt the one who hurt me. Help me have the self-control to guard my tongue in the unguarded moments.

LET LOVE LEAD YOU

"The LORD your God in your midst, the Mighty One, will save; He will rejoice over you with gladness, He will quiet you with His love, He will rejoice over you with singing."

Zephaniah 3:17

I stared at the notes from the sermon I was scheduled to preach the next day. The dark storm in our family was raging. My message was a reminder of how short life is and that we need to stop harboring resentment, bitterness and anger. The longer I stared, the louder the whisper.

Hypocrite. Hypocrite. Hypocrite. Hypocrite!

A few hours later, I had a heart to heart with a close friend. We prayed. We talked. And I was reminded of the truth. I was not a hypocrite. I was human. I was a child of God. And I was loved.

The wounds of shame can run deep. And like muddied ruts, you can get stuck in them. But I have good news for you. Shame does not have to lead you. Love can.

Love Like You've Never Been Hurt, pages 81–82

Wherever you release forgiveness, you release the power of the Spirit of God and the power of healing. Let go and let love lead you. But how do you do that? Take those thoughts captive. When you hear that name that brings up hurtful images and ill feelings, catch yourself and change that thought to a prayer of blessing over that person's life. It won't be easy at first, but if you will be more intentional about your thoughts and words, it will change the way you see everything, including yourself.

In fact, loving ourselves and seeing the best in ourselves is, for many people, the very obstacle standing in the way.

But isn't it interesting that when the Lord was asked to name the most important commandment in the Law, loving ourselves was part of the answer?

> But when the Pharisees heard that He had silenced the Sadducees, they gathered together. Then one of them, a lawyer, asked Him a question, testing Him, and saying, "Teacher, which is the great commandment in the law?" Jesus said to him, "'You shall love the LORD your God with all your heart, with all your soul, and with all your mind.' This is the first and great commandment. And the second is like it: '*You shall love your neighbor as yourself.*' On these two commandments hang all the Law and the Prophets."
>
> Matthew 22:34–40, emphasis added

Self-Talk Matters

The words you say to yourself and about yourself have far greater weight than you might imagine. *You're not good enough. You're not holy enough. You're lazy. You're undisciplined. You call yourself a Christian, and you still can't get it together.* These are some of the things I have said to myself, and I am a pastor. I know if I am saying those things to myself, then others are saying them, too. And the condemnation is beating up many good people and causing them to stop short of their callings and their purposes.

I like to say that we need to feel good about ourselves, though not in a narcissistic, materialistic or selfish way. I am talking about an unshakeable inner confidence based on what God says about us, not a distorted self-image based on what the devil likes to throw in our faces. . . . When we judge ourselves unworthy, we miss out on the treasures God has in store for us. . . . Love yourself and stay out of your own way. Sometimes your worst enemy is you.

Love Like You've Never Been Hurt, page 83

It's Not about How You See Yourself

Self-esteem is not the goal. Never has been. It's not about mirroring an image you have of yourself. Far too often *that* image is based on comparison with the world, and seldom does it reflect the image God has in mind for you. When you truly care more about how Jesus sees you than you care about how *you* see you, you will have broken through a barrier that many men and women never venture to cross.

It does not matter what you have done or what has been done to you. Jesus sees you as a wonderful masterpiece. After all, you come from a bloodline of royalty.

Love Like You've Never Been Hurt, page 85

I have said it before, and I will say it again and again. If people could ever get a true understanding of who God really is and what He thinks about them, it would forever alter the way they see everything—including those who have offended them. He is far more loving and merciful than we have imagined. He loves us with a love that is unshakable. He is *for* you. He is *so* for you.

Look at these words again:

> Who shall separate us from the love of Christ? Shall tribulation, or distress, or persecution, or famine, or nakedness, or peril, or sword? . . . For I am persuaded that neither death nor life, nor angels nor principalities nor powers, nor things present nor things to come, nor height nor depth, nor any other created thing, shall be able to separate us from the love of God which is in Christ Jesus our Lord.
>
> Romans 8:35, 38–40

You may have been sidelined. You may have been crushed by life. You may not be where God wants you to be. But you are an overcomer by the blood of the Lamb and the word of your testimony (see Revelation 12:11). If you are not there yet, hold on. God wants to make you over and show you the one He sees when He sees you, because you are always on His mind.

He Always Leads with Love

All too often, because we know the worst parts of ourselves and our sinful nature, we see God as judge and jury or the angry punishing father. We see Him with that wagging head and eyes that are filled with disappointment. But these images are of our own making and do not represent our Father in heaven.

The image you need to get set in your mind is the true image of God. His eyes are filled with love and compassion, full of grace and mercy. He is your greatest encourager. He sees the very best. Better yet, He is excited because He sees the plans He has for you and sees the potential you have inside you. He isn't the punisher. He is the skillful sculptor and the caring gardener as He prunes and shapes you for greater health and a long life. He sings over you (see Zephaniah 3:17). He is your strong tower and your place of refuge. He is with you in the valley and the one who places you on the mountaintop.

As you go to prayer today, ask the Lord to begin to show you the truth about who He is, and His thoughts toward you. Be open to an understanding of who He really is. It could make all the difference. Let love lead you . . . His love.

Prayer

Lord Jesus, You tell me to let love lead all the time. I want to live like this, and I want to love like this. I pray for opportunities this week to show love and to express love. Help me be more loving. Help me put love first in every encounter, I pray.

GET READY FOR A NEW YOU

"Do not remember the former things, nor consider the things of old. Behold, I will do a new thing, now it shall spring forth; shall you not know it? I will even make a road in the wilderness and rivers in the desert."

Isaiah 43:18–19

Society places great emphasis on external looks. Every year, plastic surgery procedures increase in number. . . . Before you start throwing some shade, this is a judgment-free zone. I am not shaming anyone who has had or is thinking of having cosmetic work done. I am sure we all have parts of our physical bodies we wish we could change. I am writing about this because I believe it echoes our spiritual condition.

Sin and shame [make] us feel ugly. So do circumstances. . . . You may feel like God's promises are not for you because your faithful prayers to break the chains of addiction seem to fall on deaf ears. If so, you need a boost. You need an extreme makeover. Luckily, we serve a God of the new.

Love Like You've Never Been Hurt, pages 86–87

Let me ask a few questions: Do you desire a new look—spiritually? Do you desire a new beginning? Do you desire a new life? Do you desire a new outlook? Do you desire a new identity? Do any of these questions resonate with you? Recovering from bad choices you have made can be a heart-wrenching experience, but God is always ready to restore you, restart your heart and help you become the "you" He had in mind when He created you.

Take a moment right where you are and look at those questions. If you have something to write with, go ahead and circle or underline the things that you desire the most. Maybe just one thing will stand out. Maybe you will circle every single question.

After you have identified which ones apply to you, I want you to do the next most logical thing you can do. Read each one out loud, one by one, and ask. Ask the Lord for a new look—spiritually. Ask the Lord for a new beginning. Ask the Lord for a new life. Ask the Lord for a new outlook. Ask Him for a new identity. Simply ask.

"Ask, and it will be given to you; seek, and you will find; knock, and it will be opened to you. For everyone who asks receives, and he who seeks finds, and to him who knocks it will be opened. Or what man is there among you who, if his son asks for bread, will give him a stone? Or if he asks for a fish, will he give him a serpent? If you then, being evil, know how to give good gifts to your children, how much more will your Father who is in heaven give good things to those who ask Him!"

Matthew 7:7–11

A sound mind, renewed mercies, forgiveness, healing and health are all yours for the asking. Strength in character and grace for weaknesses are free to those who ask. Break the chains of old thinking and be renewed in every way with one simple task—ask. And then get ready for a new you!

Get Out of the Cage

The enemy has tried hard to permanently ink you with painful memories, with failures from the past, with self-sabotaging thoughts, with fear of an uncertain future.

He wants you to always see yourself as someone who has messed up. *This is who I am. I'll never change. I'll never get healed. I'll never become whole. . . .*

Therefore, we need to feed our minds with the good stuff. When you binge on negative thinking, replaying the hurt someone caused you or the hurt you caused someone else, it becomes a habit. . . . When you start believing the enemy's lies about who you are, you begin to destroy your destiny.

Love Like You've Never Been Hurt, pages 89–90

Limiting self-talk can become a cage. And because of our human nature, we are far more prone to find a way to exist within the boundaries of the cage than imagine a life outside it. The great lie of Satan is that you have absolutely no choice about living in that cage. He wants you to believe that you are the victim in this scenario and have no way out. It is a lie. You are not the person living in that cage. But to break out, your thinking has to change, and your self-talk has to be transformed.

Renew Your Mind

The power of life and death is in the tongue, but the tongue will only say what the mind has come to believe is true. The ability to see what God is doing—and will do—for you is not always instinctual or seen by the naked eye. Those things are learned. There are powerful truths about who you are and what God has for you and even His thoughts toward you—but they must be examined and learned and understood first. Then they can be spoken by your own tongue.

> I beseech you therefore, brethren, by the mercies of God, that you present your bodies a living sacrifice, holy, acceptable to God, which is your reasonable service. And do not be conformed to this world, but be transformed by the renewing of your mind, that you may prove what is that good and acceptable and perfect will of God.
>
> Romans 12:1–2

It's about replacing your thinking with the truth of God's Word. It's about changing wrong thinking. It is about learning the truth about all things. As God's Word penetrates deep into your soul, the blood of Jesus Christ steps up from the inside with forgiveness and redemption. Get past your past by renewing your mind through the light of God's Word and through the blood of Jesus.

Our greatest battles are internal battles. If we miss the truth of God's Word, those conversations inside our minds can spiral and dump us right back into anger, bitterness, despair and isolation. This is actually pride in its most extreme form. It can be broken only with the Word of God as you learn and then proclaim the truths contained in it.

Reflect for a moment on all you have read today. And if you can say the words below to your Lord and Savior, pray them.

Prayer

Father, I forgive myself and let go of all the mistakes and sins in my life. The lessons have been learned. I forgive everyone, and especially myself. Starting today, I choose to walk in love. And I thank You for the strength and grace to do it.

HIS LOVING KINDNESS

For we ourselves were also once foolish, disobedient, deceived, serving various lusts and pleasures, living in malice and envy, hateful and hating one another. But when the kindness and the love of God our Savior toward man appeared, not by works of righteousness which we have done, but according to His mercy He saved us, through the washing of regeneration and renewing of the Holy Spirit, whom He poured out on us abundantly through Jesus Christ our Savior, that having been justified by His grace we should become heirs according to the hope of eternal life.

Titus 3:3–7

Religion points to your sin, wags its finger and says, "Shame on you." Jesus welcomes you with open arms and says, "No, shame on Me." He takes your guilt and your shame and puts it on Himself.

Love Like You've Never Been Hurt, page 95

What a drastic difference there is between being religious and having a living and loving relationship with Jesus Christ! The contrast, many times, could not be more stark. Religion finds flaws and shouts them out to the world to try to expose just how dirty you are. Relationship with Jesus says, "Of course I'm filthy. Yes, I do have flaws, and I struggle with some things, which is why my hope is in Jesus and not in my righteousness." Religion will tell you that you have to fit into its tiny box of rules and regulations about everything from how you dress to the length of your hair and what you can and can't do in a music service at church. Religion condemns and strains at gnats.

This passage shows Jesus' response to the religious of His day:

> "Woe to you, scribes and Pharisees, hypocrites! For you pay tithe of mint and anise and cummin, and have neglected the weightier matters of the law: justice and mercy and faith. These you ought to have done, without leaving the others undone. Blind guides, who strain out a gnat and swallow a camel! Woe to you, scribes and Pharisees, hypocrites! For

you cleanse the outside of the cup and dish, but inside they are full of extortion and self-indulgence. Blind Pharisee, first cleanse the inside of the cup and dish, that the outside of them may be clean also. Woe to you, scribes and Pharisees, hypocrites! For you are like whitewashed tombs which indeed appear beautiful outwardly, but inside are full of dead men's bones and all uncleanness."

Matthew 23:23–27

Whew! Could He have said it any stronger? He used those terms because that is just how dangerous religiosity and legalism can be—straining to see gnats through eyes with planks.

Jesus suggests a much kinder approach. In fact, I love this passage that talks about His kindness:

So when you, a mere human being, pass judgment on them and yet do the same things, do you think you will escape God's judgment? Or do you show contempt for the riches of his kindness, forbearance and patience, not realizing that God's kindness is intended to lead you to repentance?

Romans 2:3–4 NIV

It is His kindness that leads us to repentance. Always has been. Ephesians 4 puts it this way:

And do not grieve the Holy Spirit of God, by whom you were sealed for the day of redemption. Let all bitterness, wrath, anger, clamor, and evil speaking be put away from you, with all malice. And be kind to one another, tender-hearted, forgiving one another, even as God in Christ forgave you.

Ephesians 4:30–32

Love those last few words: *Even as God in Christ forgave you.* Funny how we want judgment for everyone but ourselves.

To Be Kind Is to Be Holy

Scripture gives a test to help you see where you stand on the forgiveness continuum. I call it *the forgiveness test.* And it is measured by the last part of the Ephesians passage above. The first part of those verses has the list of "do nots." But the second part of the passage is the list of "dos," and it serves as the test: Be kind, tenderhearted and forgiving. If you cannot be kind or tenderhearted with that person who has created the offense, then you aren't quite there with forgiveness. Keep praying. Keep loving. Keep forgiving. Keep asking for healing in that area of your life and for whatever happened that created the hurt. Love others as Christ loves you. Forgive others the way you want Christ to forgive you.

To be kind is to be holy. If you want to know how holy you are, determine how kind you are. The fruit of the Spirit is not justice, righteousness and judgment. It is quite the opposite. The fruit is love, joy, peace, long-suffering, *kindness*, goodness, faithfulness, gentleness and self-control. We don't love the way the world does with conditions and a whole set of "what ifs" and "unlesses." It is unconditional. It is the way of Jesus both in what He has commanded and in what He did under the most stressful and unjustified set of circumstances imaginable.

So many times we are in places that require open arms, grace, mercy and love. But that is hard to do with fists that are clenched, jaws that are set and arms that are folded. The law of kindness supersedes everything. The call to kindness has no boundaries. It is limitless. We Christians should strive to be warm places for those who feel lost or have been pummeled by life. Are you?

Prayer

Lord Jesus, teach me to be kind in all encounters, I pray. I desire Your loving kindness and ask You to teach me and fill me today. I pray for opportunities to show kindness this week.

BLESSED ARE THE PEACEMAKERS

The kingdom of God is not eating and drinking, but righteousness and peace and joy in the Holy Spirit. For he who serves Christ in these things is acceptable to God and approved by men.

Therefore let us pursue the things which make for peace and the things by which one may edify another.

Romans 14:17–19

Do you remember a time when you lost control of your temper? Maybe you yelled at your child, maybe even slipped in an expletive, and it frightened the living daylights out of her. Maybe you were already on edge when driving home from work; then someone cut you off and you started riding his bumper and screaming at him. Maybe after a few consecutive nights of little sleep, you blew up in a screaming fit at your spouse. Maybe you have gotten so out of control, you have done something physical, like thrown something at someone, punched a wall or smashed a window. . . .

It is normal to get angry and to want to do something about it. But we cannot position ourselves to love like we've never been hurt if we are ruled by our tempers.

Love Like You've Never Been Hurt, pages 115–116

Do you struggle with your temper? Do you know someone who does? Sometimes I think that temper and alcohol are distant cousins. Both can make us do things we never would do and react in ways we never would react. And both can cause us to go too far and say or do things we can never take back.

It is too easy to say, "That's just human nature." We have a higher calling than that. We don't have a "human" nature; we have a "spirit" nature—and the Holy Spirit lives in us. This means we will always have a check or a conviction when we are about to do the wrong thing. The

Holy Spirit sends warning signs and obstacles to impede

our progress down wrong paths and in wrong decisions. Bottom line is this: While it is not wrong to have anger at some things in this world such as crimes against children, corruption or injustice, losing your temper *always* means you are taking the reins from God and saying to Him, "I'll take it from here!"

Love Is Not Easily Angered

So many valuable character traits of the mature Christian are not instinctual. As I have said before, they are learned. They are disciplines. They are not natural reactions because they have supernatural origins. One of the greatest pieces of advice can be found in James: "So then, my beloved brethren, let every man be swift to hear, slow to speak, slow to wrath; for the wrath of man does not produce the righteousness of God" (James 1:19–20).

Proverbs says it like this: "He who has knowledge spares his words, and a man of understanding is of a calm spirit. Even a fool is counted wise when he holds his peace; when he shuts his lips, he is considered perceptive" (Proverbs 17:27–30).

Our first instinct, when challenged or angered, is not always our best response. Anger is not a sin; mismanaging it is. Take a beat and inquire of the Lord before acting—or reacting. Don't risk overreacting. Life's most regrettable moments, most of the time, could have been avoided with a cooler head.

Unguarded Moments

Oh, that life was scripted out! Oh, that we could see conflict coming, think it through, write out a thoughtful response and execute it at just the right time with just the right words! But that is not the way life works. Our most vulnerable times of conflict come in those unguarded moments—when we are surprised by a harsh word, an accusation, a bad report, news of a situation that got out of control. It's in those moments that the blood rises to the face, and we get in that fight-or-flight mode. *That* is when we need to step back, take a breath and ask the Lord for two things: wisdom and the right words. Until He gives both, it is best not to speak. Human anger does not produce the righteousness God desires. Sometimes you have to zip it and wait on the Lord. He is one step ahead of the situation, already working on your behalf. Never forget that. Be at peace when others won't be at peace with you. *You are responsible for you.*

> Repay no one evil for evil. Have regard for good things in the sight of all men. If it is possible, as much as depends on you, live peaceably with all men. Beloved, do not avenge yourselves, but rather give place to wrath; for it is written, *"Vengeance is Mine, I will repay,"* says the Lord.
>
> Romans 12:17–19, emphasis added

The Pursuit of Peace

I love these words in Proverbs: "A soft answer turns away wrath, but a harsh word stirs up anger" (Proverbs 15:1). We are called to be peacemakers. Over and over in Scripture we are admonished to play this critical role wherever we find conflict and strife, especially in the Body of Christ. "Blessed are the pure in heart, for they shall see God. Blessed are the peacemakers, for they shall be called sons of God" (Matthew 5:8–9).

Some of us are natural fighters. This is not always a bad thing, but it can be unhealthy. I'll admit, I am one of these people. If I really believe I am right on something, I will fight you to hell and back. . . .

Ask yourself this: When you find yourself in the middle of a volatile situation, how does your presence change things? Do you add kerosene to the roaring flames, or do you extinguish the fire? . . . A person who manufactures peace will defuse situations. She will not stoke the flames—she will put out the fire. . . . Peace is not the absence of trouble. . . . Peace is standing in the middle of a storm when lightning strikes . . . but you choose to be still and not panic. You choose to trust God. You choose to be at peace in the midst of a storm.

Love Like You've Never Been Hurt, pages 123–124

Be at peace when others can't or won't. Be at peace with the fact that not everyone is going to want to be at peace with you. There may be moments when your peace-making efforts are not welcome or effective. Don't live or die on the approval of others. If your self-worth and value are dependent on the opinions and acceptance of others, that is a hill you will die on many times in your life. Be at peace with an audience of one . . . Jesus.

Prayer

Lord Jesus, help me bring peace to every room I enter because I am filled with Your peace. When I encounter situations where there is strife or conflict, help me discern when to speak up and when simply to pray quietly. Give me wisdom, I pray.

LOVE GOD LIKE YOU'VE NEVER BEEN HURT

"I have told you these things, so that in me you may have peace. In this world you will have trouble. But take heart! I have overcome the world."

John 16:33 NIV

Perhaps the greatest grief one can have is over the loss of a child. While I have never lost a child, I have conducted many, many funerals for parents who have lost a child, and I have seen families completely emptied of all emotion—wrenched with grief and full of confusion. Some are angry. But most are in a state of utter shock.

What do you say at a time like this? Really, there are no words in that moment. Words will matter later, but in that moment, there are no words that bring comfort, other than the knowledge that the child is in heaven for the very young and for the older if they made a decision for Christ. Other than that, there are no words.

While I have not lost a child, I have lost a brother to cancer. I have seen hundreds or thousands of people healed from every kind of disease imaginable. I have prayed prayers of healing and faith for years and years and believed every word. I have had faith for each request. So when my brother Richie was diagnosed with cancer, there was no doubt in my mind he would be healed. But as the days and weeks turned into months, no healing came.

The day Richie died was a very difficult day for me. Not only had I lost my brother, I was struggling with the fact that God had not healed him. What do you do when there is no one to blame but God? What do you do when something terrible happens to you or a loved one or, God forbid, a child?

I am here to tell you that it is normal and understandable to question God in that moment, as you try to understand why He intervened so many times throughout history, but not for you or yours in that situation. What do you do when you are struggling with forgiveness with the God of the universe? I know of no greater test of faith than the hurt or loss of a loved one when, in your mind, it was totally preventable by a God who prevents things all the time.

God Is at the Bottom

If you have spent even one minute in a mountaintop experience, you have an entirely different perspective of the valley below. The descent—or the fall—is greatest when it starts at the top of the mountain. Being at the bottom can be overwhelming, heartbreaking and terrifying. And if we don't take some very specific steps, we leave the door open for Satan to derail us from our destinies. Too many times people have checked out right at this point in the journey, unable to make peace with the God who could have intervened. When your spirit is crushed, it can be paralyzing . . . but only if you let it.

The fact is that God has done more with people's brokenness throughout history than He has done with people who have never had to endure anything. Abraham on Mount Moriah—broken. Moses when he saw that golden calf—broken. David after he committed adultery—broken. Prophet after prophet—broken. Peter immediately following his betrayal—broken. The disciples and followers of Jesus after He was crucified—broken. And our Savior on the cross—broken . . . and poured out.

Sometimes, seasons of our greatest pain can seem like seasons of great silence from heaven. Your search for answers comes up empty, so you feel as if God's presence is nowhere to be found. But you have to know right here and right now that you were never alone for one single step. He *is* near to the brokenhearted (see Psalm 34:18). In times of grief and sorrow we can find hope in the Word of God.

God *blesses* those people who grieve (see Matthew 5:4). He helps us in our troubles so we are able to help others who have all kinds of troubles (see 2 Corinthians 1:3–4). Though we walk through the valley of the shadow of death, we will not be afraid. He is with us, and His shepherd's rod makes us feel safe (see Psalm 23:4). When we don't know what to pray for, the Spirit prays for us in ways that cannot be put into words (see Romans 8:26). Jesus knows when we are sad. But He promises that later we will be so happy that no one will be able to change the way we feel (see John 16:22). And there are many more promises in Scripture.

God Is Still God

Even in the unbearable seasons of life, He is nearer than you might think. He promises never to leave or forsake you. Keep praising. Keep worshiping. Keep believing. Keep loving. Keep forgiving. Your greatest testimony has yet to be spoken, but when it is, it will set captives free. Your sorrow will not have been for nothing.

I have learned that while God may not always offer an explanation, He does offer a promise—many promises. God knows how to make sense out of the tragedies and traumas of life. He puts to use what He has allowed you to go through, if you will place it in His hands.

Something else I have learned is another amazing truth about the way our God works. When bad becomes unbearable, good things are going to happen. Sometimes all you can do is hang on, but that is enough. Love the Lord with all your heart . . . even when it hurts. Hope is on the way.

Prayer

Lord Jesus, I love You. Even when I don't understand everything, I choose to love You and worship You anyway. You are my Lord and my Savior, and I am fully Yours. Help me understand the things I do not understand and to trust at all times.

BELIEVE THE PROMISE

Grace and peace be multiplied to you in the knowledge of God and of Jesus our Lord, as His divine power has given to us all things that pertain to life and godliness, through the knowledge of Him who called us by glory and virtue, by which have been given to us exceedingly great and precious promises, that through these you may be partakers of the divine nature.

2 Peter 1:2–4

Life is hard. We win, we lose. We love, we get hurt. We triumph, we fail. We do the right things and still experience struggle, loss, divorce, bankruptcy, abandonment, death and disappointment.

I do not know why bad things happen. God may not answer your why. Some of us may not know the purpose for our pain until we get to heaven.

Here's what I can tell you: When you are in crisis, God is not. When you are under a wave of depression, God is not. When you are lost in a valley and have no idea what to do, God has not vanished. He is still the healer. He is still the deliverer. And He is still working out a plan for your life. . . . Choose to trust Him. Choose to believe.

Love Like You've Never Been Hurt, page 191

In yesterday's devotional I talked about losing my brother Richie to cancer. And for a while after he died, I found myself shying away from talking very much about healing in my messages. I will never forget when the Lord confronted me and asked me why. I remember telling the Lord, "Because You didn't heal Richie."

And then as clearly as I have ever heard Him speak to my spirit, He said, *Make room for healing.*

And God began to heal in our services on a weekly basis. I didn't understand it, but I understood that I had to obey. Obedience is always a choice, even when grieving.

Make the Choice

We may not have any influence over the tragedies and pain we suffer, but our response to what happened is absolutely our choice. And once again, when I stop and examine the promises of God, I see that He has gone before me in every trial and every heartache. And in each place, He has left a promise:

> God will comfort you in all your troubles (see Psalm 23:4).
>
> He will meet all your needs (see Philippians 4:19).
>
> He will turn your darkness into light and make straight your crooked paths (see Isaiah 42:16).
>
> Joy comes in the morning (see Psalm 30:5).
>
> God will not forsake you (see Psalm 9:10).
>
> He will repay you for the years the enemy has destroyed (see Joel 2:25).
>
> No weapon formed against you shall prosper (see Isaiah 54:17).
>
> And because Jesus has gone and prepared a place for you, He will come again and receive you to Himself, that where He is, you will be also (see John 14:3).

The decision is yours. You can place your faith in the uncertainty of your circumstances, or you can place your trust in the promises of God. It's a choice. It is one thing to worship out of duty. It is another thing to choose to worship from deep desire when you can't find any kind of meaning in life's most difficult trials. That is an expression of complete and total dependence on Him.

> See, God doesn't take away all our troubles—at least not as quickly as we would like Him to—but He promises us peace in the midst of them. . . . It might have been a long time since you have felt God. . . . But He does promise us peace. . . . Jesus can keep you from being swallowed up [in grief and despair].
>
> *Love Like You've Never Been Hurt*, pages 195–196

It is a choice to turn your eyes away from your pain and look squarely into the eyes of Jesus. But, remember: You are in that rocky boat with the God of the wind and the waves. Trust Him in those moments, and you will find Him faithful.

Never Give Up

Here are three encouraging words.

1. You are doing better than you think. Take inventory: You have so much to be thankful for. We see what we choose to look at—what we focus on. Make the choice to see that glass half full, probably more than half full, and be thankful for all you have.

2. You matter more than you think. When things are going wrong, it is only natural to utter those three words we have all uttered: *Why me, Lord?* No matter what you are going through, God still has a plan for your life. The setback you have experienced is not a delay. If anything, it has accelerated your path. I love what that great theologian A. W. Tozer wrote in *The Root of the Righteous*: "It is doubtful whether God can bless a man greatly until He has hurt him deeply" (Christian Publications, 1955).

   There is a depth that marks the lives of those who have suffered heartache and pain. Additionally, when others are going through the worst life can throw at them, they need people who have traveled that road to help them find their way. No matter your pain, your loss or your sin, you are still what God created you to be.

3. Don't give up on God, because He has never given up on you. God is not in the business of replacing damaged people; God is in the business of *fixing* damaged people. He loves to take a tragedy and turn it into a testimony. He loves to see you triumph over life's greatest difficulties, and then watch you go back and help others through their storms. God wants to heal them, change them and transform them, and He desires to use once-broken people to reach newly broken people.

Do not give up on God, because He has never given up on you. Trust Him today. Love Him like you have never been hurt. Whatever you have gone through, this is no time to quit. Believe the promises God has declared over your life.

Prayer

Lord, when I think of the promises You have for me, and Your perfect plan, I have faith for every part. Give me patience in the waiting and help me remain continuously hopeful even when my circumstances don't seem to line up with what I have heard You speak over my life. I trust You, God. I love You and thank You for every ounce of faith You have given me.

PULLING DOWN STRONGHOLDS

For though we live in the world, we do not wage war as the world does. The weapons we fight with are not the weapons of the world. On the contrary, they have divine power to demolish strongholds. We demolish arguments and every pretension that sets itself up against the knowledge of God, and we take captive every thought to make it obedient to Christ.

2 Corinthians 10:3–5 NIV

DAY 17

I come with a prophetic word today over your life and your future. Where you are is not your final destination. God is calling you to a place greater than where you are. God has not destined your life to be filled with constant conflict or hurt or shame. See these times of difficulty for what they are. These are seasons of growth and shaping and not life sentences. God has destined you for victory in every area of your life.

The Bible talks about strongholds. These are places where the enemy has focused attention, effort and forces to defend and maintain his position. For some it may be an addiction, while for others it is a secret sin. For some it is an offense that just cannot be let go. Scripture shows us that these are seats of authority in high places. But just as the above verses declare, we have weapons—spiritual weaponry—whose express purpose is to pull down those strongholds and demolish them. That's in your Bible.

What the Enemy Is After

So what does this have to do with you? With each new offense, coupled with every old offense, multiplied by every bit of bitterness you harbor against someone who hurt you, inch by inch Satan builds a stronghold in your life that you will not be able to overcome by normal means.

What does this mean for you? It means that the things you have been going through are not always God's way of shaping you. Many times they are Satan's way of derailing

101

you, getting a lock on your destiny and purpose, and throwing away the key. When we rage or exact revenge through gossip or harsh words, we open that door for the enemy to come in and set up residence. A stronghold.

> When the enemy comes against you, he is after something. He does not just pick on you to pick on you; he is after the spoils. . . . He wants to take you and the ones you love and infect them with bitterness, unforgiveness, anger and offense.
>
> *Love Like You've Never Been Hurt*, page 207

Don't let him win. Don't let him in. This is why forgiveness is so important. This is why it is critical that you love like you've never been hurt. There is an enemy looking for just a crack in your faith, just a crack in your armor to be able to get a foothold. And footholds lead to strongholds. Don't let him in.

> You may be facing a stronghold in your life. Maybe you are trying to save your marriage. Maybe you are trying to salvage a relationship with a wayward adult child. However big or intimidating the stronghold, God can set you free. . . .
>
> I do not know how dirty your battle has gotten. But I do know that it is the very place where God will be glorified the most in your life. It is where the anointing will come through.
>
> *Love Like You've Never Been Hurt*, page 208

Don't Settle

If there is anything I have learned about my walk with Christ, it's that I cannot trust my eyes when trying to discern God's presence in my life or my progress along the path. When I look only at my circumstances, I think I am not making any progress at all, while in the spirit, I am exactly where I am supposed to be . . . right in the middle of my next growth cycle.

It may not look like a growth cycle with human eyes because all they see is another trial or challenge. But, in the spirit, it's my next step. It's a new lesson that teaches me where I need to grow or a challenge that stretches me. I can complain, or I can take a deep breath and inquire of the Lord. Then, one day at a time, I keep walking, using the lessons from the past combined with my faith for the future.

God is with me. God is with *you*. That's all you need to know. He is *for* you, and He is growing you into the person you need to be for that next assignment. Trust Him. Walk it out. Stay steady. He's got you. Pray those strongholds down. Proclaim God's promises over your life . . . out loud. Call down the armies of heaven when you feel overwhelmed. And take every step forward with the confidence you would have if you knew God was standing right beside you for every challenge . . . because He is.

Prayer

Lord Jesus, teach me how to do battle in the unseen world. Give me the courage to pull down strongholds, and fit me with every piece of spiritual armor I need. Help me to be fearless as I face those evil forces in my life. You are my strong tower and my very present help in time of need. Thank You for Your protection.

FAITH IN THE UNSEEN

Now faith is the substance of things hoped for, the evidence of things not seen. For by it the elders obtained a good testimony. By faith we understand that the worlds were framed by the word of God, so that the things which are seen were not made of things which are visible.

Hebrews 11:1–3

Are you responding to what you see or to what God says? Think about it—really think about it. When you look at what lies around you, do you feel pressure? Do you feel overwhelmed? Do you feel fear? Defeat?

Scripture is clear that faith has nothing to do with what we see. We walk by faith, not by sight (see 2 Corinthians 5:7). Faith comes by hearing, not by seeing (see Romans 10:17). . . .

If you listen, you will hear God telling you that He is on your side, that He is fighting for you, that with Him you are more than a conqueror.

Love Like You've Never Been Hurt, page 212

The Bible actually makes it even clearer than that when it says in Hebrews 11:6 that *without faith, it is impossible to please God*. Impossible. Think about that. If it is impossible to please God without faith, then it stands to reason that we are all going to have situations, on a regular basis, where faith is required. And, further, faith will never be required unless there is a situation that tells you it can't be done, and yet you feel it is exactly what you are supposed to do. Faith.

This tells me that in every case where you suffer an injustice, you will be tested. You will have to choose between exacting your own justice or trusting that God will avenge and provide justice, whether you ever get to see it or not. Faith.

Faith isn't just that train going up the hill saying, "I think I can, I think I can." It's so much more than that.

It's refusing to waver on decisions you *know* the Lord led you to make, even though you can't see how it's all going to work out.

Giving: God's Faith Test

I think an area where people really struggle with faith is in the area of giving. Better yet, people struggle in their faith with tithing, which is giving ten percent of their income. And here is where it gets really interesting. Most people don't struggle about whether or not they are supposed to tithe; they struggle with *doing* it. And these aren't bad people! They are simply people who can add and subtract. And on paper, giving ten percent of their income means something doesn't get paid. Their eyes and their logic say it's not possible.

But eyes tell lies because they can't see the spiritual; they can see only the physical. All the while God has a different kind of math that says, "Give Me the ten percent tithe, and I will help you do more with ninety percent than you ever could have done with the full hundred percent." Tithing is hearing with your ears and not trusting your eyes. Faith.

Believe what God says, about everything, and not what you feel or what your circumstances dictate. Ask yourself this question constantly: With each new decision, am I responding to what I see or to what God says?

Monkey Business

Another area where faith is required is in forgiveness. In some countries, monkeys are used for food. In fact, monkey brains are considered a delicacy. But monkeys are extremely hard to catch. At least they used to be. Then one day, people discovered that once monkeys get hold of something in their hands, regardless of how meaningless the thing is, they won't let anyone take it out of their hands. Well, with this information, one wise tribesman decided to put salt or seeds in the carved-out holes in large rocks. Once the monkey's hand was in the hole, the tribesman would jump out and scare the monkey, causing it to close that fist on the seeds. Then, capturing the monkey was as easy as could be.

Crazy that all the monkey had to do was let go of the seed, and he would never be caught. I have often thought how similar we are to those monkeys. There are names and faces that carry offense or hurt toward us in the past that we simply will not let go of. We hold on to these people with such great fervency that no one can cause us to release them. And, in doing so, we have been successfully trapped. We can't go anywhere or do anything. We are easy for Satan's capture simply because we refuse to let go.

I said it before, and I will say it again. Withholding forgiveness is like drinking poison and expecting the people we are angry with to get sick. The only ones we are hurting are ourselves. But we would rather hold on than trust God to deal with those individuals. That's not just an obedience issue; it's a faith issue. Faith.

You Have Faith for This

If you have not figured this out yet, life is an uphill climb. On your way to the place, the purpose, the destiny or the high place that you are trying to reach in life, it is going to require some climbing. . . .

God is looking for climbers. Climbers are dedicated. They face risks. They stare at mountains that look insurmountable. And they accept God's assignment to climb and conquer those mountains in His name.

Love Like You've Never Been Hurt, page 214

Faith. To every person there is given a measure of faith. "For I say, through the grace given to me, to everyone who is among you, not to think of himself more highly than he ought to think, but to think soberly, as God has dealt to each one a measure of faith" (Romans 12:3).

God has given *you* a measure of faith. And the measure you have been given will always be enough. Whatever your circumstance—you have the faith for it. Whatever command from God's Word you are struggling with—you have the faith for it. Whomever you need to forgive—with God's help, you have the faith for that, too. Trust Jesus and His word in all things. All.

Prayer

Lord Jesus, teach me to use the faith You have given me. Remind me, Lord, of all the times You have been faithful to me and of the many times You have delivered me. Help me connect Your faithfulness in the past to my present-day struggles as I learn to trust You anew each day.

DAY 19

QUITTING IS NEVER AN OPTION

And let us not grow weary while doing good, for in due season we shall reap if we do not lose heart. Therefore, as we have opportunity, let us do good to all, especially to those who are of the household of faith.

Galatians 6:9–10

As I prepared to write *Love Like You've Never Been Hurt*, I studied the story of elite Navy SEAL Marcus Luttrell, winner of the distinguished Navy Cross. His story of survival in Afghanistan is remarkable. But the story within the story is the insight he provides about what it means to be a Navy SEAL.

One part of Luttrell's story really caught my ear, and made me think of everything we have been talking about for the last eighteen days of this devotional. He tells how the men who enter the Navy SEAL program are highly skilled individuals and some of the toughest men in the world. Yet the training is so rigorous that two thirds who start never finish the course. He tells in *Lone Survivor* (Little, Brown, 2007) how one of his instructors gave him these profound and very applicable words for his journey: "The body can take . . . near anything. It's the mind that needs training."

As I wrote *Love Like You've Never Been Hurt*, I thought about my journey. And I thought about the people who would read that book or walk through the 21 days of this one. "It's the mind that needs training," the SEAL instructor said, adding, "Can you handle such injustice? Can you cope with that kind of unfairness, that much setback? And still come back with your jaw set, still determined, swearing you will never quit?"

When you have been praying for your family, for your marriage or for God to heal that broken relationship, there are times you may feel like giving up. [You have] the option to quit. All you have to do is say, "I'm tired of the battle and I'm giving in."

Love Like You've Never Been Hurt, page 217

I want to challenge you right now to remove the quit option from your life.

Therefore do not cast away your confidence, which has great reward. For you have need of endurance, so that after you have done the will of God, you may receive the promise. . . . "Now the just shall live by faith; but if anyone draws back, My soul has no pleasure in him." But we are not of those who draw back to perdition, but of those who believe to the saving of the soul.

Hebrews 10:35–36, 38–39

Never Back Down

We are not of those who draw back. *You* are not of those who draw back. *You* are one of those who receive the promise! We are in a battle for our lives. Like Navy SEALs we fight, but ours is a spiritual battle.

Finally, my brethren, be strong in the Lord and in the power of His might. Put on the whole armor of God, that you may be able to stand against the wiles of the devil. For we do not wrestle against flesh and blood, but against principalities, against powers, against the rulers of the darkness of this age, against spiritual hosts of wickedness in the heavenly places. Therefore take up the whole armor of God, that you may be able to withstand in the evil day, and having done all, to stand.

Ephesians 6:10–13

The battle is not what we see in the natural. The battle is not about the trouble in your family. It is not about the financial problem. It is not about the sickness. It is not about the disagreements in your marriage. The enemy wants your mind. He wants to break you down mentally. He wants you to give up, to quit, to say, "I can't take this anymore!"

Love Like You've Never Been Hurt, page 217

In your daily quest to finish the race and to believe the promises of God, you can never, ever—can I say *ever*?—forget that there is an enemy. That enemy has one goal: to get you to ring that bell of surrender.

But I come with good news! The battle has already been won. Satan is a defeated foe, and he knows it. We go from victory to victory and glory to glory! The outcome is never in doubt, and the best news ever is this: "Greater is He who is in you than he who is in the world" (1 John 4:4 NASB). You were made to overcome. You were made to thrive. You were designed to live a victorious life.

Bold Proclamation for a Victorious Life

I will never quit. These need to be your words, and they need to be repeated often.

If you get knocked down you *will* get back up—because that's not just what you do, it's who you are. You *are* an overcomer. You *are* victorious. You *are* the head and not the tail. You *are* above and not under. This world is *not* your home. You have a *great* hope and promise in Jesus. You *will* pray for your enemies. You *will* bless those who curse you, because you see a much bigger picture than the one a momentary offense paints for you. You *will* get to God's house and worship with your church family. Your family *will* be saved, and they *will* walk and talk with their God. You *will* thrive in your work. And you *will* love the Lord your God with everything in you.

Pause and reflect on that last paragraph. Take it in and hold it in your heart for a moment. Now take a minute to go back and proclaim out loud each of those statements of faith—only this time personalize each statement. Replace whatever words are needed to make each statement your own. It is not enough simply to know these things. You take these statements to a whole new level when you proclaim each one out loud—speaking truth and life over yourself. Take the time now, and take it often.

Prayer

Lord Jesus, please help me remove the word quit *from my mind. Help me remain steadfast in the face of every opposition and every hurt. Help me to cast my cares on You. You are my peace, Lord. Help me remember that, in every stressful situation.*

AFTER THIS—THERE'S MORE

For I know the thoughts that I think toward you, says the LORD, thoughts of peace and not of evil, to give you a future and a hope. Then you will call upon Me and go and pray to Me, and I will listen to you. And you will seek Me and find Me, when you search for Me with all your heart. I will be found by you, says the LORD.

Jeremiah 29:11–14

God's grace is enough. His love is enough. His anointing is enough. Friend, your destiny is greater than your difficulty. Your destiny is greater than your disaster. Your destiny is greater than your present dilemma. Your destiny is greater than your fears. . . . Proverbs 21:30 [NLT] says, "No human wisdom or understanding or plan can stand against the LORD." . . .

No knowledge, no power, no wisdom, no strategy and no counsel will come against God's purpose and plan and win.

Love Like You've Never Been Hurt, page 223

Heaven is fighting for you! "There is no wisdom or understanding or counsel against the LORD. The horse is prepared for the day of battle, but deliverance is of the LORD" (Proverbs 21:30–31).

God is never out of resources or options. The only option was given on a cross more than two thousand years ago. And with that one sacrifice sin was paid for. Then, three days later, death and the grave were conquered, and victory was won.

Forever and ever.

Now, allow me to take it even deeper. Have you ever paused to think that the God of the universe desires to talk to you today? Can you fathom that the very same Jesus we sing about, the same one in the Bible, desires to spend very intimate time with *just you*?

We spend a great amount of time thinking about offenses and hurts—eyes always looking out at people and down at our circumstances. We need to shift our focus, to turn our gaze away from all of that, and place it straight on our best friend, our redeemer, our advocate, our teacher and our champion: Jesus.

Courageous Considerations

I have both a statement and a question for you.

> *Statement:* You are as close to God as you choose to be.
> *Question:* What would one five-minute conversation with Jesus right now do for the rest of your day?

What would just a few minutes wrapped in His love and affection do for your sense of worth and value today? Right now? How would one moment in His actual presence impact your spirit right now? Do you realize there is not one thing I have said in this paragraph that is not possible, right now, right where you are? The access granted to you to approach the very throne of God is both breathtaking and almost unfathomable, and yet there it is. Freely given by a God who has waited all week to see you.

To have more of Jesus in you is to have more and more of His perspective on your problems and your challenges. To experience His forgiveness for your sins creates greater capacity in you to forgive others. To look deeply into His Word and gain His mind and His comfort for your greatest **119** tragedies and your deepest hurts not only helps you deal with them yourself, but it enables you to be a carrier of light for others who are living in those dark places of despair . . . in desperate need.

That is just how near your God is. That is the access that is legally and rightfully yours as a Christian.

After This

Two of the most powerful words found in Scripture for people who have suffered great loss can be found in the book of Job. After he had gone through more tragic loss than anyone in his time, we see this simple passage that means everything. These two words have tremendous impact: "*After this* Job lived one hundred and forty years, and saw his children and grandchildren for four generations" (Job 42:16, emphasis added).

I don't know what all you have been through, and I would never seek to minimize anything that has fallen to you to bear. But one thing I can promise. When the dust settles, there will be an "after this." God has an "after this" for you. There are chapters left in your life to be written.

You may have lost a loved one. You may be dealing with a broken relationship. You may be wrestling with an addiction in your family, or you may even struggle with one yourself. God has an "after this" for you. You are going to get through your struggle. . . . You are going to live after your loss. You are going to live after your betrayal.

Love Like You've Never Been Hurt, page 225

It's Not Over

I believe you are reading this devotional today by divine appointment. God wants to tell you, "It's not over." What a powerful thought! What a powerful truth! There is a "next" in your future, and God wants to make every painful moment you have experienced count for the Kingdom. It was *not* all for nothing. If you will loosen your grip and give Him whatever happened, He will take what Satan meant for evil and use it for good. "But as for you, you meant evil against me; but God meant it for good, in order to bring it about as it is this day, to save many people alive" (Genesis 50:20).

Just as we have talked about, it is not enough simply to read and agree and move on. If you want a powerful truth to get down into your spirit and affect the way you see God and the world you live in, then you need to get in the new habit of proclaiming truths *out loud*. You have to proclaim: I *do* have full access to the throne of God. I *am* as close to the Lord as I choose to be—and I own that. There *is* an "after this" for me. I need to begin to shift my focus off my past and allow God to show me my future. Because if I ask, He will. It's *not* over.

Prayer

Lord Jesus, I am filled with excitement about the future because all things "next" are in Your hands. Help me shift my focus off my past and place it on all things "after this." Help me renew my thinking and my purpose.

PULLING IT ALL TOGETHER

And not only that, but we also glory in tribulations, knowing that tribulation produces perseverance; and perseverance, character; and character, hope. Now hope does not disappoint, because the love of God has been poured out in our hearts by the Holy Spirit who was given to us.

Romans 5:3–5

DAY 21

Here we are at Day 21!

By now we have agreed that loving others is not always easy, but it is who we are, and it is what we do. Not just because it's a good idea, but because God commands it, His Son, Jesus, lived it and it's the best spiritual medicine we can take to cure the deepest of wounds. But it's more than that. Without the opposition of offenses, you and I will never mount up with wings like an eagle.

> Offenses are inevitable. No one is exempt. One way or another, we are all going to get offended, get hurt, get insulted, get betrayed, get cheated, get shamed, get violated or lose our pride.
>
> Since being offended is a biblical fact, we must learn how to deal with it. . . .
>
> Some of us look at opposition as a bad thing. And certainly, it can feel that way. But opposition can be an opportunity. Think of it this way—without the opposition of offenses, you will never mount up with wings like an eagle (see Isaiah 40:31). Without opposition, you will never soar. . . .
>
> Opposition can cause you to face things and do things you could not have done, had you not had the opposition. Opposition will make you pray. Opposition will make you come running to God. Opposition will make you increase your faith.
>
> You may need to start seeing those who offend or hurt you as an opportunity for God to take you higher.

Love Like You've Never Been Hurt, pages 228–229

I love this poem from *Leaves of Grass* (Thayer and Eldridge, 1860) because it explains these things profoundly, the way only Walt Whitman could:

> Have you learned lessons only of those who
> admired you, and were tender with you, and
> stood aside for you?
> Have you not learned the great lessons of those
> who rejected you, and braced themselves
> against you? or who treated you with contempt, or disputed the passage with you?

We have covered a lot of ground. This devotional was written about ten months after *Love Like You've Never Been Hurt* was released. Because of my opportunities to speak about that earlier book, I hear feedback from all over the world. This feedback isn't about people telling me they enjoyed the book; it's about the way they have begun to walk out the principles of love and forgiveness. The testimonies bring me to tears each time I hear them. Families healed, marriages restored, friendships renewed through forgiveness.

I have learned anew, through principles in Scripture and principles the Lord gave me on my own personal journey, that God provides the very thing hurting people need the most: how to love like they've never been hurt. It *is* possible to forgive even the worst hurts.

I want to encourage you to go deeper in your relationship with Christ even as you continue to put into practice what you have learned in these 21 days.

God does His most stunning work where things seem most hopeless.

Love *never* fails.

It is *never* wrong to love people who have messed up.

It is unforgiveable not to forgive.

To love others, we must first learn to love ourselves.

We are called to be kind.

Be a peacemaker; it's our calling.

Faith resides in the unseen.

We *can* love like we've never been hurt.

Quitting is *never* an option.

After this, there's more.

Right now the Holy Spirit is pulling into your driveway. He is coming for you. . . . It is time to restart your heart. . . . God knew years ago that you would be where you are right now. Trust Him. He has already prepared the way for you.

Love Like You've Never Been Hurt, page 230

Never forget: God is so much nearer and so much more accessible than you have ever imagined. Make the time to draw near every day. Allow God to restart your heart. And start to love like you've never been hurt.

Prayer

Lord Jesus, thank You for every word of encouragement, every lesson learned and every new perspective. Thank You for Your Holy Spirit, and thank You for everything that is to come next. I trust You, Lord, with an unshakable trust. And I love You with every bit of love that is in me. Heal me where healing is needed. Help me extend forgiveness where forgiveness is required. Help me to love again—and not just with any love, but with love like I have never been hurt.

Jentezen Franklin is the senior pastor of Free Chapel, a multicampus church. Each week his television program, Kingdom Connection, is broadcast on major networks all over the world. A *New York Times* bestselling author, Jentezen has written nine books, including his most recent *Love Like You've Never Been Hurt*, the groundbreaking *Fasting* and *Right People, Right Place, Right Plan*.

Jentezen and his wife, Cherise, have been married 31 years, have five children and four grandchildren, and make their home in Gainesville, Georgia.